Drawings

Jean Dubuffet

Introduction by Virginia Allen

The Museum of Modern Art, New York

Distributed by New York Graphic Society Ltd., Greenwich, Connecticut

Gift of Mr. and Mrs. Lester Francis Avnet

Undaunted by the vagaries of aesthetic trends, Jean Dubuffet has continued to draw throughout his artistic career. He destroyed most of his work done before 1942, but one of the few surviving examples, a realistic sanguine drawing of his grandmother done in 1921 when he was nineteen years old, already indicates the assurance of his draftsmanship. Returning to art in 1942 after an interim career in the wine business, he has continued to intersperse his painting, printmaking, and sculpture with periods of intense drawing activity.

Because of its great versatility and variety of materials, drawing can be different things to different artists: a proving ground for new ideas; a means for rapidly recording images to be elaborated later; a medium for preparatory study; occasionally an independent art form whose only *raison d'être* is its own existence; and, rarely, the consummation or synopsis of an aesthetic already fully expanded in painting or sculpture. Dubuffet's drawings have traditionally been placed in the latter category, but, in truth, such generalization is impossible. While the "Corps de dame" and "Texturology" series come chronologically after the related paintings, others do not. During three visits to the Sahara Desert, Dubuffet filled eight notebooks with sketches and completed a number of small drawings in gouache, watercolor, and distemper, but returned to the convenience of his Paris studio to paint. Similarly, he did his second series of experimental ink imprint assemblages when he first moved to Vence in January 1955, primarily because limited studio space discouraged painting. Therefore, external circumstances motivated at least two exceptionally productive drawing episodes, both of which preceded the paintings of the same series.

The thirty-nine remarkable drawings reproduced here, acquired for The Museum of Modern Art by Mr. and Mrs. Lester Francis Avnet, were originally in the collection of the art dealer, collector, and connoisseur Daniel Cordier. In 1956, Cordier bought four hundred black-and-white drawings and gouaches from Dubuffet's atelier, to which he gradually added later drawings purchased directly from Dubuffet himself. Setting aside eighty or ninety, he began to sell the rest. The collection was amassed with love and sensitivity—for drawings in general and those by Dubuffet in particular—so it is hardly surprising that the quality is uniformly superb. Among the Museum's Dubuffet drawings are examples from most of his major series, which provide the opportunity to examine in depth the whole range of his draftsmanship. From such a study comes the inescapable conclusion that unpredictability and duality are among the few constants in Dubuffet's work. As it undergoes metamorphosis from restrained to frenetic, line alternately defines and obliterates solid form. Objects dissolve into texture, only to reappear in different guise. Table tops tilt to reveal, not the still life that Cubism has conditioned us to expect, but the teeming activity of a micro-landscape. The subject matter is as varied as Dubuffet's treatment of it, traversing man, his machines, and his activities; nature, from grandiose to microscopic; and animals.

Like Picasso, Dubuffet frequently returns to earlier thematic concerns. Eight-and-a-half years of rapidly changing styles separate *Evolving Portrait* (page 24) and *Figure with Hat in a Landscape* (page 25), but the visual similarities attest to Dubuffet's frequent stylistic recapitulation. Both figures function as shapes against which the busy linear patterns are played. The fluid ink line swells and thickens, then dwindles to a mere trace along a seemingly meandering and sporadic course. In actual fact, the boundaries established by the contours of the figures are rigidly observed, thereby imposing strict discipline on the frantic linear activity. Both drawings are composed of minute, frequently autonomous components that can be read independently. Particularly in the earlier drawings, Dubuffet traces the portrait with faces, figures, insects, numbers, and letters.

Despite pronounced similarities, there do exist the important differences one would expect to find in two drawings separated by almost nine years. Immediately apparent is the change in background treatment. The unrelieved expanse of white paper surrounding the figure in *Evolving Portrait* ties both figure and background firmly to the picture surface. By extending the internal configurations to the surrounding environment in *Figure with Hat in a Landscape,* Dubuffet achieves the finely balanced ambiguity and interaction between figure and background that is typical of his later work. The figure is readable as three-dimensional form through concentration of ink around the contours, but it is simultaneously and inexorably tied to its surroundings. Both figures suffer Job-like afflictions, but the first braves only a surface invasion of pests that in no way penetrates the flat, impassive facade; the second figure is consumed with the decay of its encroaching environment, which leaves it decimated and pathetically naked. Not surprisingly, the earlier drawing is more open, almost frivolous, in technique. The second is more condensed, inviting close scrutiny. Although "portrait" and "figure" are both unnamed, the two drawings are dissimilar in their anonymity. "Portrait" is of no one. It is, furthermore, non-human. Its shape, although vaguely recognizable as a head and shoulders, is purely object. The second figure is terrifyingly human and becomes Everyman in its implications of universal vulnerability.

Eight drawings from the 1940's document the emergence of Dubuffet's interest in the art of the naive and untrained. In drawings by children, mediums, prisoners, and mental patients, and in the graffiti scrawled by anonymous, often earthy artists on backstreet walls, Dubuffet found a refreshing alternative to several established aesthetic values that he considered arbitrary.

> The idea that there are beautiful objects and ugly objects, people endowed with beauty and others who cannot claim it, has surely no other foundation than convention—old poppycock—and I declare that convention unhealthy....I would like people to look at my work as an enterprise for the rehabilitation of scorned values.[1]

Nearly a hundred portrait-drawings from this formative period embody Dubuffet's extraordinary aesthetic. Thirty-five of them were exhibited with related paintings at the Galerie René Drouin in October 1947 under the banner Vive leur vraie figure. For the most part, these were portraits of Dubuffet's friends, among them the Surrealist sculptor Michel Tapié (page 3, top) and the painter Jean Fautrier (page 3, bottom). The Visitors Welcomed (page 5) and Desert and Bedouin (page 4) recall the frontally conceived stick figures and simplified delineation of children's drawings, while Figure (page 2) and the two Metro drawings (pages 6 and 7) are scratched and scraped into the surface of prepared pasteboard in the manner of wall graffiti. Not surprisingly, Dubuffet's search for a naive pictorial vocabulary that would circumvent the artifice of an acquired culture led him to admire the work of Paul Klee. The highly experimental Shadows Cast in the Pine Forest (page 1) approaches complete mental abstraction, and of all Dubuffet's drawings it is perhaps the most reminiscent of Klee.

Throughout the year 1950 Dubuffet was occupied with one of his major series of paintings, drawings, and lithographs, "Corps de dame." Through his grotesque treatment of that most sacred of aesthetic objects, the female nude, Dubuffet continued his war against conventional beauty. Whereas the painted nudes assault our sensibilities with bizarre tonalities and monstrous anatomical deformations, the drawings are less disturbing, for two reasons. The fifty-three drawings (see pages 8, 9, and 11) fall late in the series, after most of the paintings had been completed, and Dubuffet's exhaustive reworking of the theme through thirty-six paintings doubtless produced the complete familiarity with subject that often culminates in unconscious stylization. In addition, his transition to the "cooler" medium of black ink on white paper precluded the surreal color palette and emotion-charged hacking and gouging of the picture surface possible with oil paint.

With the "Corps de dame" drawings begins a peak period of linear activity. Evolving Portrait (page 24) and Bowery Bum (page 13), which were done in New York, and Table Laden with Objects (page 20, left), which was done in Paris, further extend the frenzied automatism begun in the "Corps de dame" series. The busy botanical and geological compositions of "Radiant Lands" (see pages 14, 15, 16, and 17), the next major series of drawings, dating from June to October 1952, also spring directly from the internal scribblings of "Corps de dame."[2] Woman Ironing a Shirt, I (page 12), an unusual drawing done as an exercise in restricted delineation, is, by contrast, extremely stylized and controlled. Five detailed and precise pastoral drawings represent this second aspect of Dubuffet's linear development. His frequent visits to the rural surroundings of Clermont-Ferrand during the summer of 1954 reawakened his interest in nature; from this period come the "Cow Grass, Foliage" drawings and paintings (see pages 18, top, and 19). Similarly, Post at the Foot of a Wall (page 21), Donkey and Cart (page 18, bottom), and Tree (page 20, right) were inspired by the rural setting of Vence, where Dubuffet established a permanent studio in April 1955.

Just as the "Corps de dame" drawings anticipate "Radiant Lands," so "Radiant Lands" contain the seeds of the

1958 "Texturologies." "Radiant Lands" exposed a cross-section of earth swarming with life both above and below ground; the "Texturologies" subject minute portions of this slice of landscape to microscopic examination. The two drawings reproduced (pages 22 and 23) date from November 1958, not only after Dubuffet had been painting texturologies for nearly a year, but also after he had begun his related, mammoth lithographic project, "Phenomena." Recognizing the fundamental "painterly" quality common to both media, Dubuffet constructed the lithographs and the paintings of minute, overlapping areas of color, or of vague black-and-white textural patterns. His progression to pen and ink dictated a return to the linear vocabulary never completely absent from any of his drawings.

Of primary interest in the three drawings of July-August 1960 (pages 25, 26, and 27) is Dubuffet's reintroduction of the human figure into a landscape left unpopulated during the preceding two years. He has said, "It seems to me that in the whole development of my work there is a constant fluctuation between bias for personages and bias against them."[3] Within a background of dots and dashes condensed from the landscape techniques of "Radiant Lands" and "Texturologies," these personages herald the floating figures-in-landscapes of the series "One Episode from 'Legends': Exodus" (see pages 32 and 33 and frontispiece). Of all the drawings illustrated, this group is the most painterly. Line is all but drowned in dense, black wash. With the addition of linear crosshatching and the colors red and blue, these jagged, angular personages will in turn become the series "L'Hourloupe." Indirectly, Dubuffet's reinstatement of the human figure spawned the major series of paintings and drawings that was to occupy most of his time during 1961-1962. Entitled "Paris Circus," the series is closely related in spirit and imagery to the 1943-1944 "Views of Paris." Two automobile drawings (pages 30 and 31) represent Dubuffet's in-depth, witty probing of Parisians and their activities.

Dubuffet's development as a draftsman has been self-perpetuating, for as surely as one group of drawings evolves out of the preceding series, it also anticipates the one to come. He thinks and works in series. No sequence of drawings is without its counterpart in another medium, and generally the major series in all media coincide and interact. During his explorations of a given subject, Dubuffet moves from drawing to painting, from lithography to sculpture and back again, with the insatiable appetite of one whose total absorption is too great to be contained within the confines of any one medium. He makes no distinction between media on the basis of importance, and recognizes no limitations other than the changes in approach dictated by the materials themselves. Dubuffet has said that his paintings and drawings alike are "usually done in the same spirit of research and experimentation..."[4] In truth, drawing is frequently the pivotal force in his total artistic development. From each series of drawings emerges a new approach to be investigated, for, as Daniel Cordier has said, "They are a sort of meditation, leading him to new experiments through the stimulus of a change in size, tools, and materials."[5]

1. Landscaped Tables, Landscapes of the Mind, Stones of Philosophy (New York: Pierre Matisse Gallery, 1952), [p. 3].
   Reprinted in Peter Selz, The Work of Jean Dubuffet (New York: The Museum of Modern Art, 1962), p. 64.
2. Daniel Cordier, The Drawings of Jean Dubuffet (New York: George Braziller, Inc., 1960), caption for plate 23.
3. "Statement on Paintings of 1961," letter to the author, in Selz, op. cit., p. 165.
4. "Memoir," in ibid., p. 106.
5. Op. cit., [p. 1].

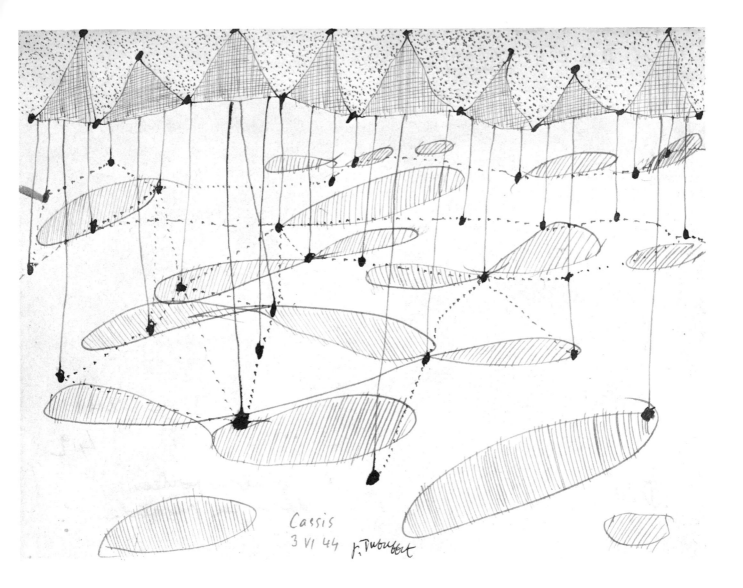

Cassis
3 VI 44   J. Dubuffet

1

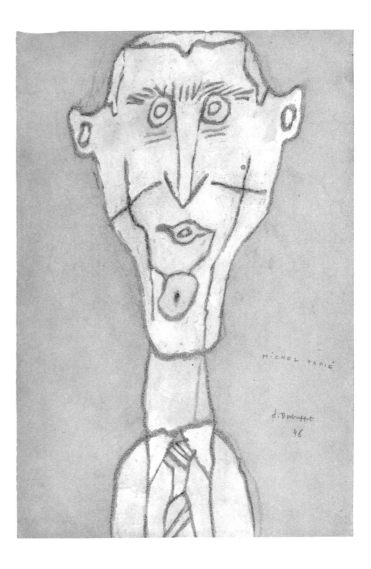

MICHEL TAPIÉ

J. Dubuffet
46

FAUTRIER

J. Dubuffet
47

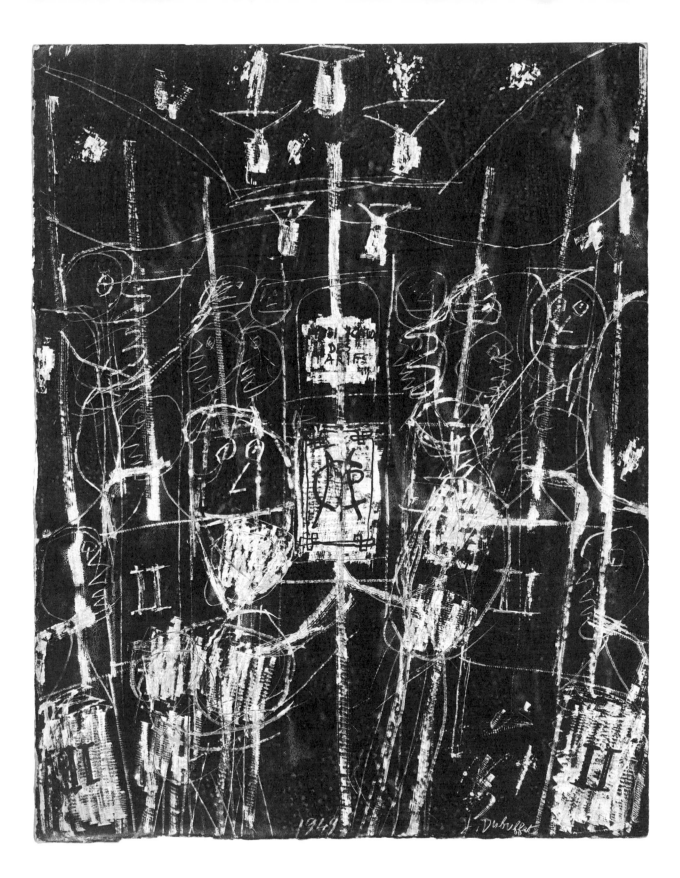

9

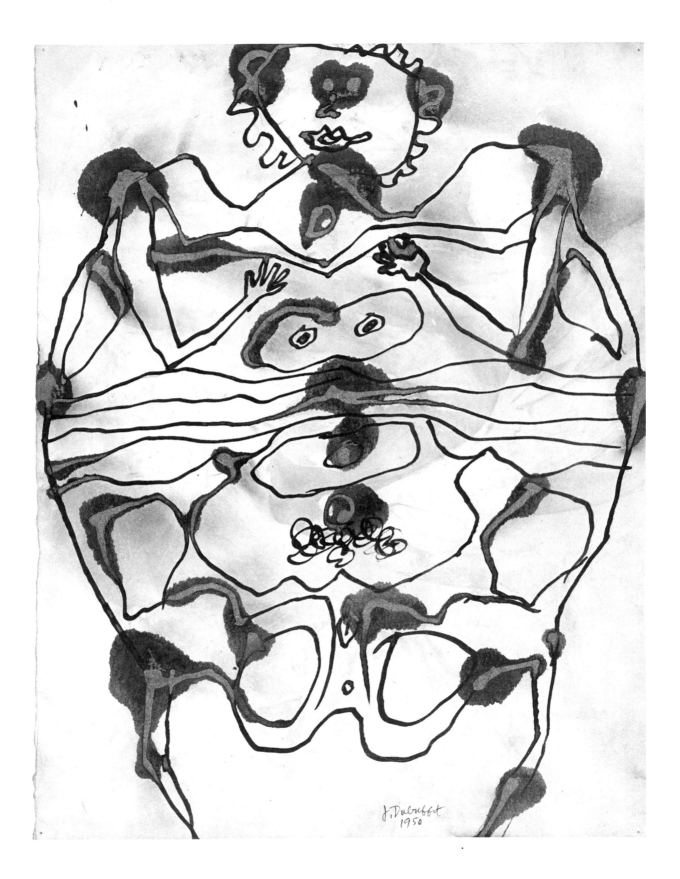

11

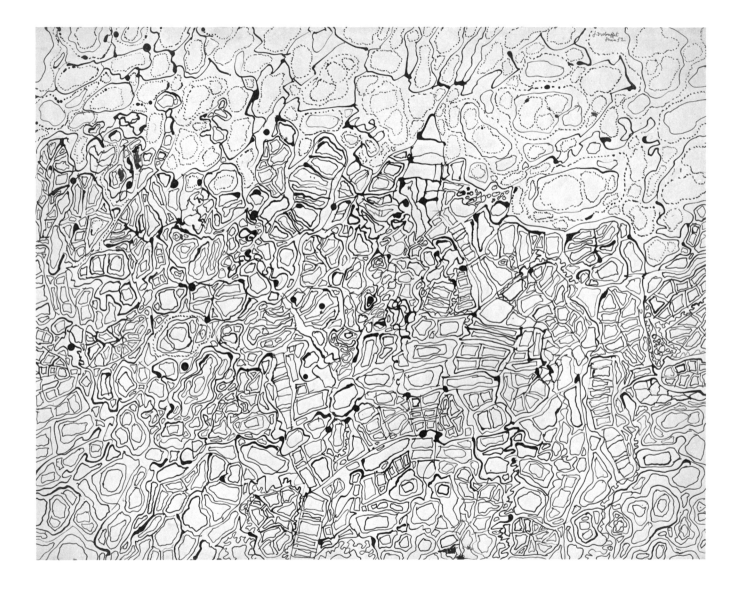

14

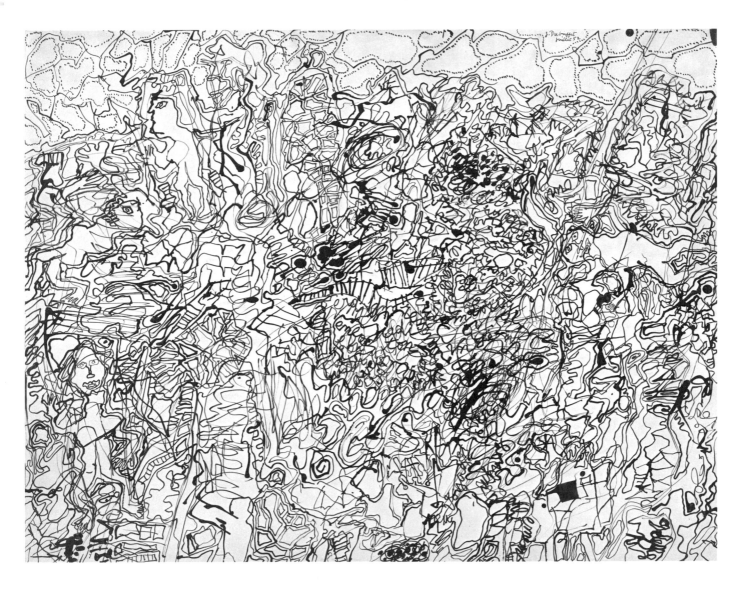

15

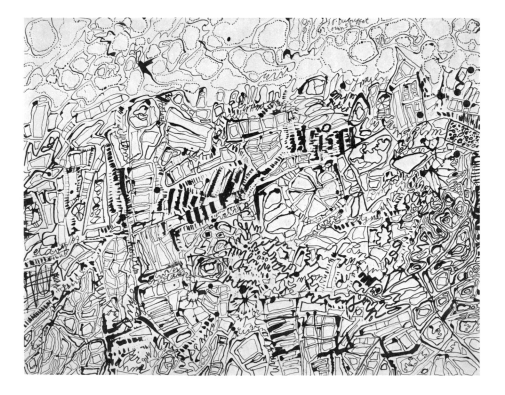

16

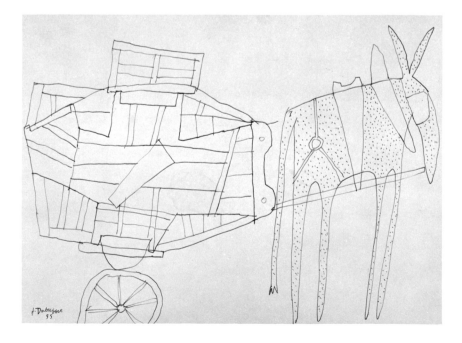

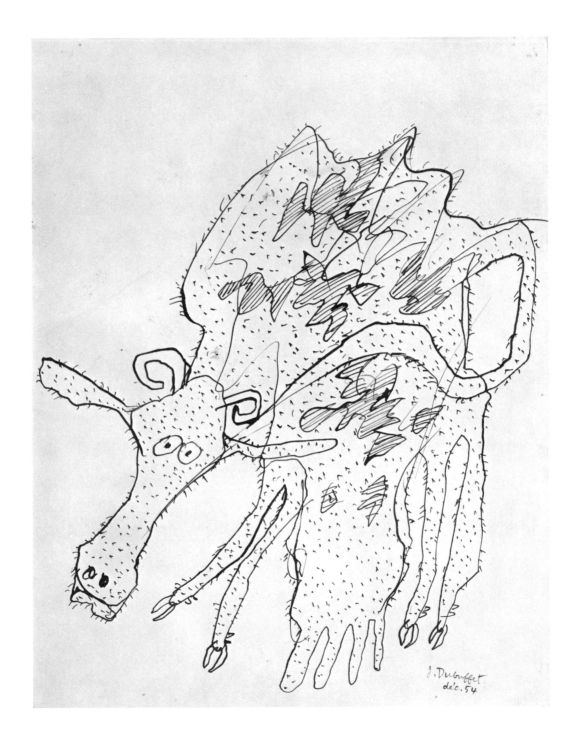

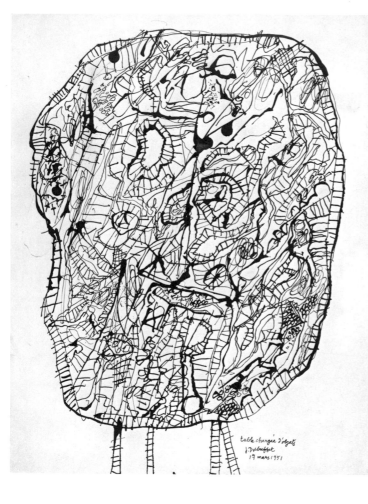

table chargée d'objets
J. Dubuffet
17 mars 1951

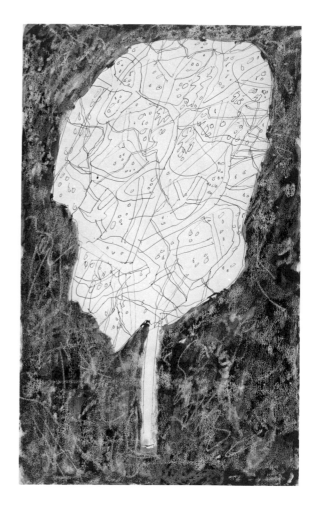

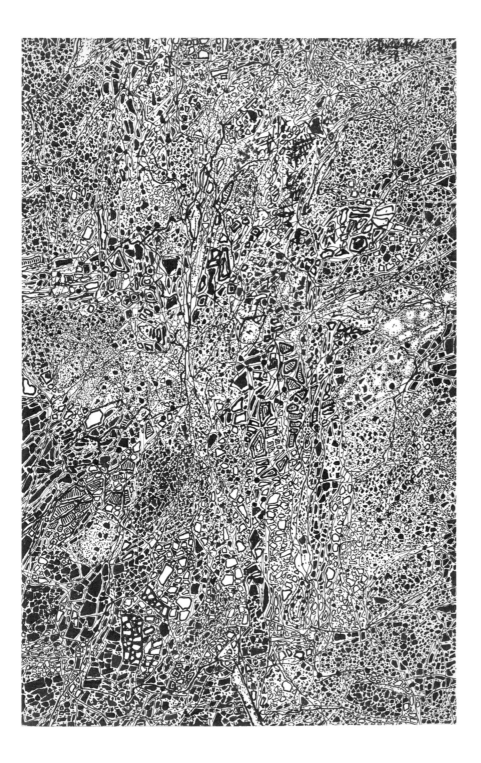

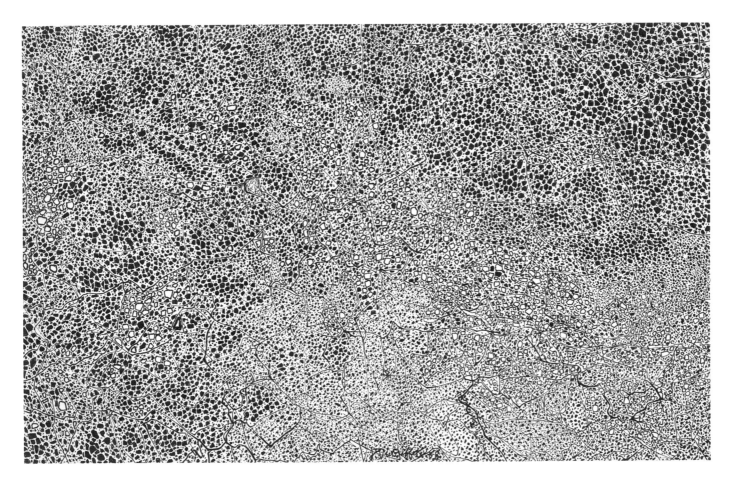

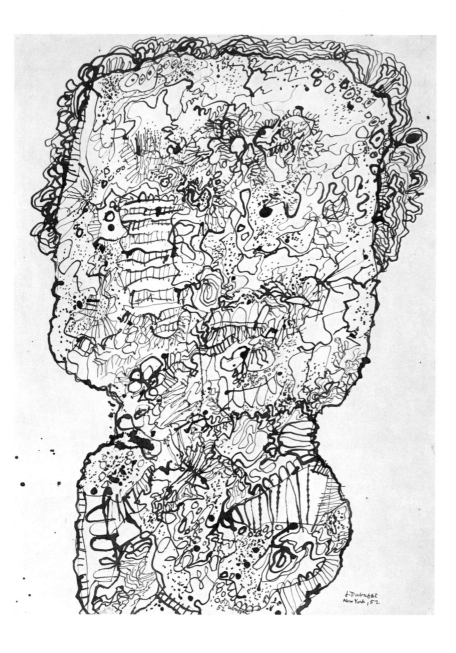

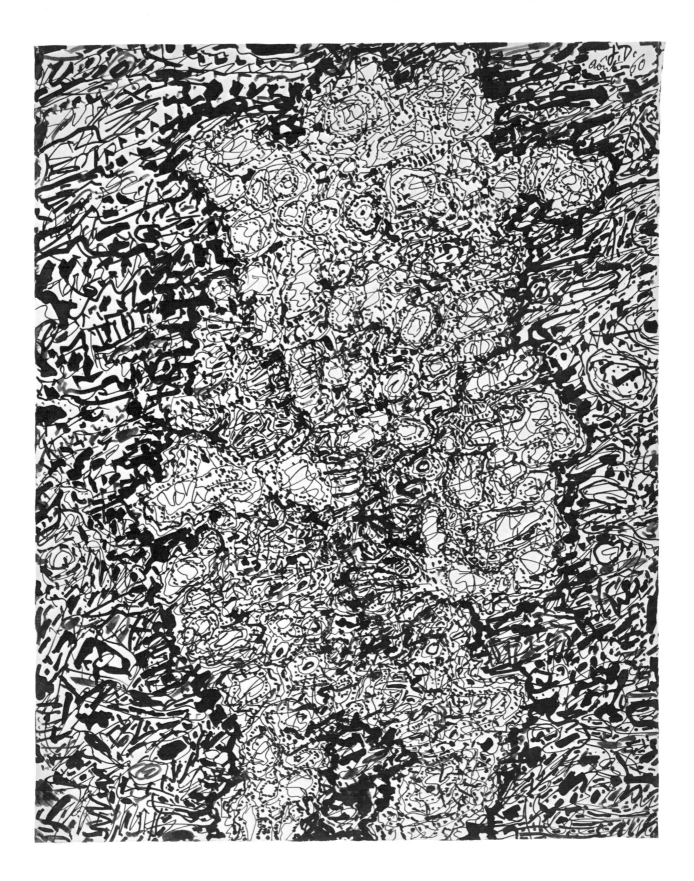

25

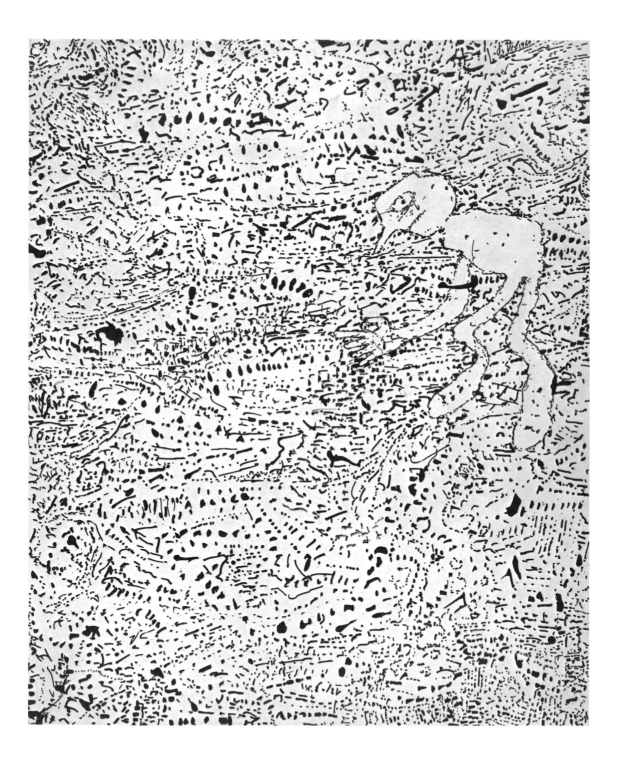

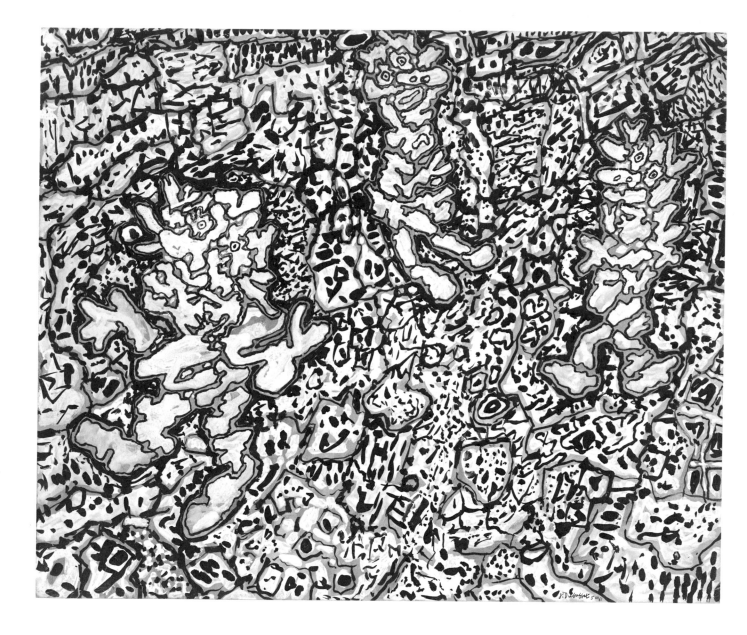

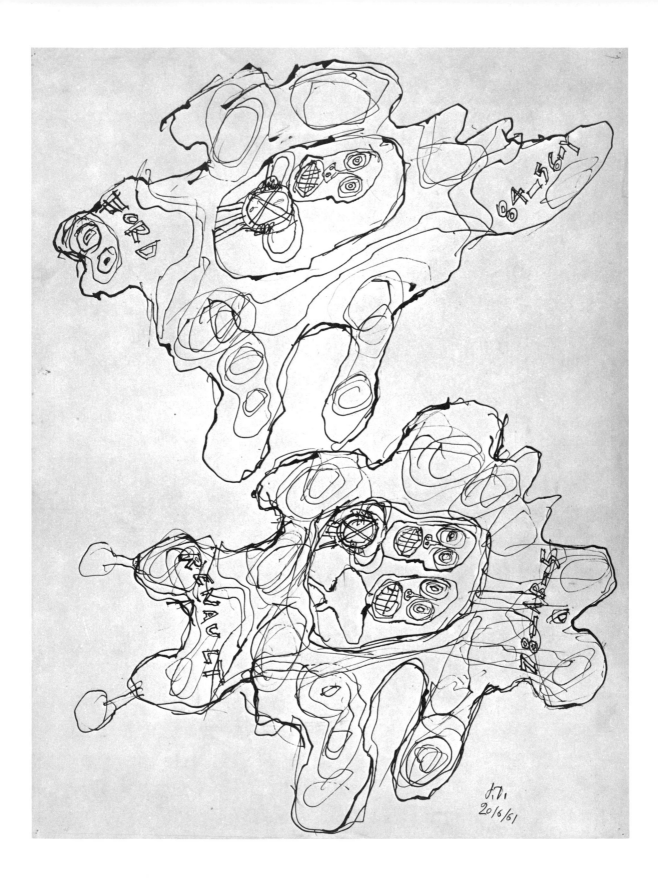

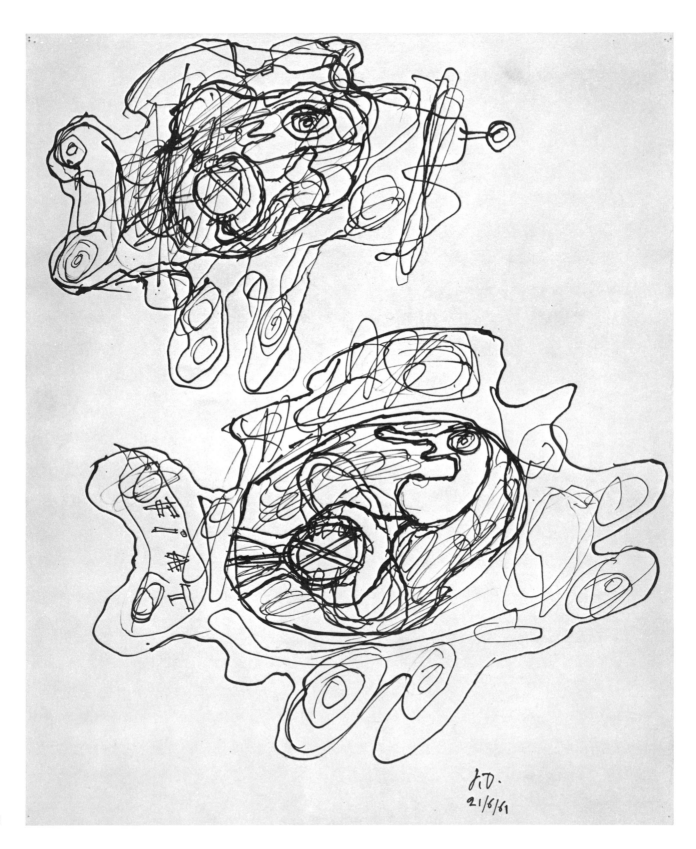

31

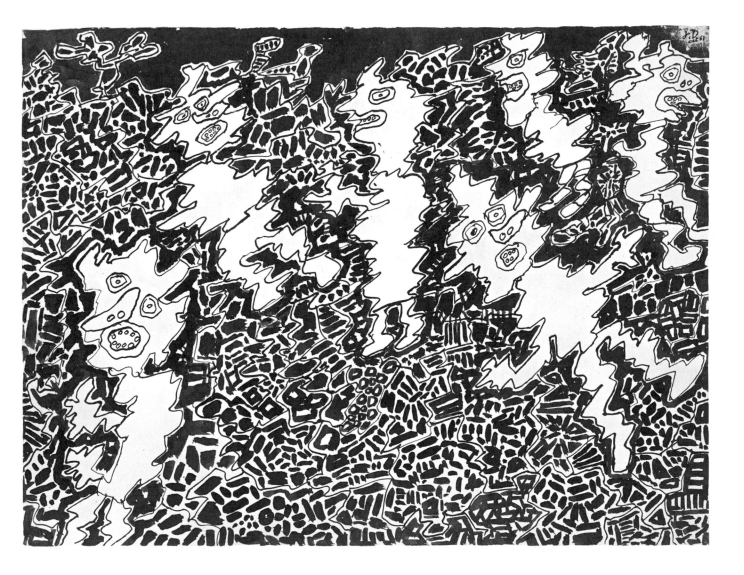

33

These thirty-nine drawings by Jean Dubuffet (French, born 1901) were acquired for The Museum of Modern Art by Mr. and Mrs. Lester Francis Avnet. In the listing below, the page number of the illustration precedes each entry. Occasionally, titles are not translated because of their idiomatic usage, or to avoid repetition. Dates enclosed in parentheses do not appear on the works themselves. In the statement of dimensions, sheet size is given in inches and centimeters, height preceding width. "L" refers to Max Loreau's definitive *Catalogue des travaux de Jean Dubuffet* (Paris, Jean-Jacques Pauvert, thirteen volumes published from 1964 to date).

from the series "One Episode from 'Legends': Exodus"
("Un épisode des légendes: Exodus"):
Frontispiece
Figure, Black Background (Personnage fond noir).
3 October 1961. Brush and pen and ink, 13¼ x 9⅞ inches
(33.5 x 25.0 cm.). L.XIX, 185.

Page 1
Shadows Cast in the Pine Forest (Ombres portées dans la pinède). Cassis, 3 June 1944. Pen and ink, 5⅜ x 6⅞ inches
(13.6 x 17.5 cm.). L.I, 265.

Page 2
Figure (Personnage). 29 June 1944. Incised ink on gesso
on cardboard, 11¼ x 6⅝ inches (28.3 x 16.7 cm.). L.I, 296.

from the series "More Beautiful than They Think: Portraits"
("Plus beaux qu'ils croient: Portraits"):
Page 3, top
Michel Tapié. (August) 1946. Gouache and charcoal, 16⅜
x 10⅞ inches (41.6 x 27.5 cm.). L.III, 11.
Page 3, bottom
Jean Fautrier. (July-August) 1947. Pen and ink, 10⅝ x 8¼
inches (26.7 x 20.9 cm.). L.III, 140.

from the series "Roses of Allah, Clowns of the Desert"
("Roses d'Allah, clowns du désert"):
Page 4
Desert and Bedouin (Désert et Bédouin). (El Goléa,
January) 1948. Pen and ink, 12⅝ x 9¼ inches (31.9 x 23.4
cm.). L.IV, 210.